The
CREATOR'S
KIDS

The CREATOR'S KIDS

Written by Nicole Helm

Illustrated by Boyana Atwood

NEW YORK

LONDON • NASHVILLE • MELBOURNE • VANCOUVER

The Creator's Kids

Published in New York, New York, by Morgan James Publishing. Morgan James is a trademark of Morgan James, LLC. www.MorganJamesPublishing.com

Proudly distributed by Publishers Group West®

Morgan James BOGO™

A **FREE** ebook edition is available for you
or a friend with the purchase of this print book.

CLEARLY SIGN YOUR NAME ABOVE

Instructions to claim your free ebook edition:
1. Visit MorganJamesBOGO.com
2. Sign your name CLEARLY in the space above
3. Complete the form and submit a photo
   of this entire page
4. You or your friend can download the ebook
   to your preferred device

ISBN 9781636982427 paperback
ISBN 9781636982434 ebook
Library of Congress Control Number:
2023939124

Cover Design by:
Boyana Atwood

Interior Design by:
Chris Treccani
www.3dogcreative.net

Morgan James is a proud partner of Habitat for Humanity Peninsula
and Greater Williamsburg. Partners in building since 2006.

Get involved today! Visit: www.morgan-james-publishing.com/giving-back

For Halle and Noa -
Go after your dreams.
Shine your light.
You're loved.

I am who God made me to be.

Romans 8 : 38 - 39

He loves me
beyond belief.

I am full of laughter like Sarah.

Tickle your belly.

Genesis 12 - 23

I am brave like Daniel.

Daniel 1 - 12

Do your
superhero pose.

I am honest like Hannah..

1 Samuel 1 - 2

Point to your mouth.

I am loving like Ruth.

Ruth 1 - 4

Give yourself a hug.

I am strong like Samson.

Show off your muscles.

Judges 13 - 16

I am trusting like Mary.

Fold your hands to pray.

Luke 1 : 26 - 56

I am joyful like Paul.

Smile as big as you can.

I am kind like Joseph.

Give yourself a high five.

Genesis 37 - 50

Judges 4 - 5

I am a leader like Deborah.

Stand up as tall as you can.

I am smart like
Solomon.

Make your thinking face.

I am a good listener like Noah.

Put your hands
behind your ears.

Genesis 6-

I am patient like Esther.

Check your
imaginary watch.

Mark 10 : 13 - 16

I am enough because I am created in the image of God.

Point to Jesus in
your heart.

Thank you, God, for loving me and making me who I am meant to be.

About the Author

Nicole Helm is a Christ-follower, wife, mother to two sweet girls, and newly added author to her title. She is surprised that she is finally using her English degree! Nicole was born in Washington State, currently living in the Midwest, but her heart is in South Carolina. Travel, home design, and reading fill her free time. She founded The Creator's Kids Co. to help parents intentionally teach their children about Jesus. Find out more via her website www.creatorskidsco.com and on Instagram @creatorskidsco.

About the Illustrator

Boyana Atwood is a bestselling author of *Pray with Me* and *Bible Verses for Toddlers* who has recently added "illustrator" to her job description. Boyana's creations are inspired by her experiences with Jesus, and her travels around the world. Born and raised in Serbia, Boyana completed her education in Switzerland, where she worked in a major bank as a Client Advisor. She then moved to Dallas, TX, where she attended Christ for the Nations and met her husband.

Together, they traveled to Mozambique and the Philippines as missionaries. Eventually, they settled in Alaska, where they now live with their three precious children. Find out more about Boyana on Instagram at @highbridge.art or search for her books on Amazon.

Craft and Activity Ideas

Free download of 12 fun craft and activity ideas focusing on the 12 characteristics in the book: www.creatorskidsco.com/products/craft